Giving Cookies and Love

♥♥♥♥♥

Grace Earline Campbell

New Hope
Birmingham, Alabama

New Hope
P. O. Box 12065
Birmingham, AL 35202-2065

© 1998 by New Hope Publishers
All rights reserved. First printing 1998
Printed in the United States of America

Dewey Decimal Classification: 259
Subject Headings:　　　MINISTRY
　　　　　　　　　　　CHURCH WORK

Scripture quotations are from the Holy Bible, King James Version.

Cover design by Cathy Lollar
Cover photography:
Pupil of the Eye Photography/John Schoenfeld

ISBN: 1-56309-249-2
N983118•0598•5M1

To order New Hope products or for a free catalog, call 1 (800) 968-7301. Also visit our web site at www.newhopepubl.com.

Introduction

❤❤❤❤

And the King shall answer and say unto them, Verily I say unto you, Inasmuch as ye have done it unto one of the least of these my brethren, ye have done it unto me (Matt. 25:40).

Giving Cookies and Love is a complete resource guide for anyone who is interested in starting a cookie ministry. It includes everything necessary to begin a unique ministry to share Jesus with others. This is my personal experience with a rewarding ministry of baking cookies and sharing God's love with others.

The best cookies are the result of using all the necessary ingredients and following a recipe. A cookie ministry is the same way. You need all the proper ingredients and the directions found in this book. Here you will find the recipe for an effective ministry with many ideas for churchwide, group, and individual participation. I have tried the suggestions in this book, and they will work in the real world.

Giving Cookies and Love is an answer for anyone looking for a new ministry idea. Read carefully each step and responsibility for the various ministry projects. The specific projects described in this book are unique, yet similar. Following the steps and responsibilities as outlined will insure a successful ministry. Choose a ministry that involves the whole church, a large group, a small group, or take the ministry on by yourself; whatever will work best in your situation and for the project you choose. You can bake the cookies in your church's kitchen or participants can bake cookies in their homes. Many people may want to participate but not have confidence in their cooking. Others may not have time to bake cookies when they are needed. However, there is a place in a cookie ministry for everyone who wants to participate. Suggest that inexperienced bakers use refrigerated dough from the dairy case of the grocery store. Encourage others to help make cookie carriers, package the cookies for delivery, and/or deliver the cookies to their destination.

As you read each chapter of this book and see the need to begin a cookie ministry in your community, my prayer is that you will hear the Lord speaking to you. Seek His guidance about where He wants you to begin your ministry. Be ready and willing for God to use you whatever your circumstance. Share this book with your pastor, minister of education, senior adult minister, Sunday School teacher, or others on the church staff who are interested. Cookie ministries have brought me many joys and great blessings. I wish for you the same delight and fulfillment that I have experienced.

The following is a list of some of the joys I have experienced in leading cookie ministries.
- Volunteers have told me that they will bake cookies as often as they are needed.
- Many people have asked for their names to be added to the list of volunteer bakers.
- I received a personal letter of appreciation from a man at New Hope Home.
- I was presented with a certificate of appreciation from the Waterfront Rescue Mission.
- On one occasion, all the men at New Hope Home signed a thank-you card for the bakers.
- College students have sent thank-you letters.
- The manager at a local Ronald McDonald House sent a Christmas card and a thank-you message.
- My pastors and members of church staffs have supported and encouraged me and the volunteers in each of the churches where I have established cookie ministries.

Definition of a Cookie Ministry

What is better than eating cookies? For me it's giving them away, and I do this through a cookie ministry; reaching out to others with cookies and love. I have found that when people receive cookies as a gift, they see my love and concern for them. As Christians, we can show our love to others in many ways. A unique way to share our love with others is through a cookie ministry. This ministry combines love, giving, and cookies to reach out to others with love.

Lottie Moon, a missionary to North China between 1873 and 1912, may have begun the first cookie ministry. In order to be a friend to the Chinese people and share Jesus with them, she first reached out to the children. She remembered the warm, sweet smell of home baked cookies and how much she had loved eating them as a child. She thought the Chinese children would like some home baked cookies, too. Through the years, she baked hundreds of American tea cakes for the Chinese children. Lottie Moon's cookie ministry opened the door for many new friendships. When she became friends with the children, she also became friends with the children's mothers.

A gift of home baked cookies says someone cares. However, baking cookies for someone else is a great way to brighten your day as well. Ministering to others by giving them cookies provides you with a blessing beyond measure. It is a ministry that you can carry with you wherever you go. Wherever you live, someone needs cookies and love.

A cookie ministry is adaptable to many situations. It can be a churchwide ministry, and it is ideal for a small group within a large church. A Sunday School class can begin a cookie ministry. Two or more women can get together each month, bake cookies, and take them to people in the community. And, if the situation warrants, one person can conduct a successful cookie ministry by herself. Everyone can participate in some way.

Whatever size of ministry you choose, you need to elect a chairperson to be responsible for obtaining permission to provide cookies for nursing homes, college students, hospital waiting rooms, and so forth. This person will also be in charge of getting volunteers to bake, package, and deliver cookies.

A group who choose to provide cookies for a hospital emergency room once a month will need permission from the hospital administrator or public relations director to begin the ministry The group will need only one person per month to bake three or four dozen cookies. If there are six active women in the group, each woman will need to bake cookies only twice a year. Place baked cookies in a cookie tin to keep them fresh, and deliver them to the hospital.

A Sunday School class may decide to have a quarterly ministry, or the whole church may decide to provide a cookie ministry during special holidays. The women can bake cookies and go as a group to visit people and distribute the cookies. Men and children can participate in this ministry, too. You may choose to go to a children's home, women's shelter, or a nursing home. The chairperson should obtain permission to visit and give cookies to the selected site. She should set a time and day for your visit and find out how many cookies to provide. Don't forget to ask about anyone who is on a special

---

Lottie Moon Tea Cakes
⅔ cup butter
2 cups sugar
3 beaten eggs
1 teaspoon vanilla
6 cups flour
½ teaspoon soda
⅔ cup milk

Cream butter. Gradually add sugar until creamy. Add eggs and vanilla. Mix well. Sift flour and soda together. Add to creamed mixture alternately with milk. (Dough will be soft.) Roll out thinly on a floured surface. Cut dough with a floured knife into squares. Bake on a lightly greased baking sheet about 8–10 minutes in a 375° oven. This recipe makes about 5 dozen cookies.

diet and cannot have cookies. Provide sugar free candy, fruit, or other special treats for people who cannot eat sweets.

A cookie ministry is a good ministry for teenagers. They can get together and bake cookies at one of their homes or at a leader or teacher's home. Each person could be in charge of bringing one or more ingredients for the cookies. The adult who is overseeing this project needs to be sure that all ingredients available, just in case someone forgets to bring the assigned ingredient. It is always better to have extra ingredients than not enough. Bake plenty of cookies, so teenagers can eat some, too. Encourage the teenagers to go as a group to share the cookies with people in their community. They my choose to give cookies to homebound people in the neighborhood, children at a children's home, and so forth.

Do the project that works best for your church and your group. Whichever ministry you decide, people will know that others care for them. Everyone involved in this ministry will receive a blessing and have lasting memories.

Senior adults will enjoy participating in a cookie ministry, too. They can bake cookies at home and bring them to the church at a specified time. Each person can help package the cookies and prepare them for delivery to the ministry site. This can be a ministry for a small class or entire senior adult department.

A group may choose to provide cookies for the people in a nursing home. The chairperson is responsible for contacting the activity director of the nursing home for permission to give cookies to the residents. The director can tell how many cookies will be needed and if there are residents who need sugar-free treats. The group can decide if they will visit the residents and deliver the cookies or choose one person, perhaps someone who already makes regular visits to the nursing home, to deliver them. The nursing home director may prefer to distribute the cookies during a meal or snack time.

For each project, groups can decide if the cookies should be packed in individual bags, large plastic bags, boxes, or containers. One or more people should be assigned to pack the cookies. If needed, make sure there are plenty of resealable plastic bags. Someone who does not have time to bake cookies may be want to be in charge of furnishing the bags. Try to make all your plans at one meeting and make the assignments well in advance of baking and delivery times.

Consider using the church kitchen for this ministry. The chapter titled Baking Cookies at Church gives the details. Does your church have other outreach ministries to the community? If the pastor or lay members lead Bible studies in nursing homes, jails, or prisons, consider adding cookies to this ministry.

A cookie ministry can begin with any number of people willing to bake cookies, but there must be a leader. Every church will always have women willing to bake cookies. Small ministries are just as important as large ones because lives are being touched. You may never know how many people were touched because you or someone in your church gave cookies to an unchurched person. A cookie ministry will show the love and concern of your church as they reach out to others in your community or city. These people in your community will remember your church in a special way.

Although some of these cookie ministry projects are not geared for individuals to personally sharing their love one-on-one with others, they are still showing love and concern for other people. As your church reaches out to others in your community, it shows people that you care about them. Through this love and concern you may meet many spiritual needs.

Through a cookie ministry you can make a difference in someone's life. Will it be a visit and cookies to a local nursing home or children's home? Will you bake cookies and drop them off at the emergency room of your local hospital? A college, children's home, or a homeless shelter may not be in your hometown, but there is someone waiting for your cookies and love.

Remember God calls us to serve Him in many ways. If you like to bake cookies and give them to others, you can begin a ministry. Give a copy of *Giving Cookies and Love* to your pastor, church staff, and friends. Ask for their prayers and support as you begin your ministry. One woman willing to begin a cookie ministry can make a difference and touch the lives of many people.

Love and Cookies
♥♥♥♥♥

A heart full of love

A mind full of concern

Your inner soul full of prayer

Ears for listening for guidance

Arms for reaching individuals

Hands for giving

Fingers for touching lives of others

A mouth for telling others about Jesus

Legs for walking this path of service

Feet for putting your prayers into action

Combine all ingredients

Follow the instructions of *Giving Cookies and Love*

You will have an effective cookie ministry

Earline Campbell

Ministering with Cookies

There are a variety of ways to minister to others with homemade cookies. Some of these ministries are twofold where you give cookies and visit individuals such as people in a nursing home. Here you have the opportunity to meet the people and talk with them. If you conduct this as a monthly ministry, you can get to know the people and have opportunities to witness to them.

You may decide to take cookies to a particular place such as a hospital waiting room. Most often you will not have an opportunity to visit with cookie recipients. In this case, you can include a card with the name and telephone number of your church. (A sample page of church calling cards is in the chapter titled Baking Cookies at Church.) People will know who provided the cookies as well as have the name of a place where they can turn for help, advise, or a friend. Others will know that your church has this ministry and can help them begin a ministry like it in their church. Your ministry can grow and reach many people in different ways.

I hope by sharing my ministries, you will receive insight for beginning a ministry in your church. I conducted some of these ministries in my small church of about 200 members. We began with three women who baked cookies to take to a local nursing home. One of the women was 90 years old. Although she was older than most of the nursing home residents, she enjoyed baking cookies and sharing her love.

My present church has more than 4,500 members. Almost 150 individuals are a part of the cookie ministry. Most of the women bake once or twice a year. And, yes, several men sign up to bake cookies, too. Some people bake cookies regularly and others choose to bake only as they are needed. Since I like to bake cookies, I bake them every month. I arrange the names of the bakers in alphabetical order, then I choose about 24 people to bake cookies each month. You may prefer to let people sign up for the month of their choice. At my church, we provide cookies each month for five different groups of people. Sometimes we take cookies to an additional organization such as the children's home, or we participate in a group ministry with other churches in the city. We also bake cookies for new families who move into our church's temporary houses.

The size of your congregation will usually determine the number of volunteers who are willing to bake cookies. The larger your church, the larger the number of volunteers you will have to bake cookies. The number of volunteers will help you decide which organization or group of people to provide cookies for. Where you live will also be a determining factor of what projects you can take on. I have had unique opportunities for ministries in different churches and areas where I live. As you read the following pages, my prayer is that you will seek out unique opportunities that fit your situation and learn of a ministry close to your heart.

Hospitals

Hospitals have surgery, outpatient surgery or emergency waiting rooms. Everyone has probably sat in a hospital waiting room at one time or another. Sometimes the hospital provides coffee for the family members who are waiting. Homemade cookies will add to the taste of the coffee, and weary families will appreciate your thoughtfulness.

Wherever you live, there is usually a hospital near your home or church. Large cities have several hospitals. Call the administrator or public relations director of the hospital nearest your church for approval to begin a cookie ministry for a waiting room. Ask the administrator to decide which waiting room will be best for the ministry.

Only provide about four dozen cookies, because they may not have storage space for more. Arrange the cookies in a cookie tin or on a heavy paper plate wrapped with a foil or plastic wrap. Or, you may choose to use a shoe box lined with foil or attractive tissue paper for a container. Include in the container a small card with the name and telephone number of your church.

If you are assigned to take cookies to the surgery or outpatient waiting room, take them early in the morning (between 7:00 and 8:00 a.m.). If a church member works at the hospital or if someone passes the hospital on their way to work, ask them to deliver the cookies for you. Coordinate your plans on when and where to pick up the cookies and deliver them. This person may not have time to bake cookies but can play a vital role in the ministry.

Late evening or night is a good time to take cookies to the emergency room. Families coming in during the night will appreciate the cookies. Consider taking cookies on a Sunday afternoon, or choose one evening during the week to deliver them. Try several times to see which one is best for your group and for the emergency room. The hospital ministry is a good monthly ministry for a church of any size. It also makes a good beginning ministry, because only a few people will need to bake cookies. In some cases, you may need only six people to bake cookies twice a year. This small number of people can make a big difference in your church and your community. Hospital staff, patients, and families will know your church as a caring church.

College Students
Do you live in a college town? Colleges are wonderful places for cookie ministries. Contact the dean of students and ask for names of the directors of Christian organizations on campus. These people can provide you with information about special events or times when cookies would be especially appreciated. They know about students who are experiencing homesickness and others who are feeling the pressures of college life. Through your cookie ministry you will find many students with no church affiliation. Many students come to know Jesus as their personal Savior during their college years. Your cookie ministry could be a positive influence on these young lives.

Contact the directors of Christian organizations, and tell them about your cookie ministry. Explain how it works and how you can give cookies and love to college students. Offer to provide cookies for special meetings, when students are studying for final exams, or other occasions. Ask the directors how many cookies will be needed, when, and where to deliver them. Ask the directors to tell the students that the cookies were provided by your church. The students will learn that your church is a caring church that reaches out to others.

A cookie ministry to a college campus is an ideal ministry for any size church. Mothers who have children away at college are usually eager to bake cookies for students. A large church can take on this kind of ministry as a monthly project. A small church may choose to provide cookies only during special holidays such as Easter and Christmas or when students are studying for final exams. Whether you take on a monthly ministry or one geared toward special events, be sure to take several bags of cookies; college students will eat more than you think! Include a small card with the name and telephone number of your church with each bag.

Students often travel to attend retreats, conferences, or on mission trips sponsored by the Christian campus organizations. Your church can provide cookies for them to eat while they travel. Ask the directors of these organizations for specific dates. You will need to deliver the cookies the day before the students leave, since they may be leaving before daylight. Work out with the director the best way to deliver the cookies. Your church can bake enough cookies to provide plenty of snacks, easing the spending cost of the trip.

International College Students
Many international college students are in the United States temporarily. They return to their country when they complete their education. Some bring family with them while others travel alone. Many internationals have different backgrounds, cultures, and religions than the American students. These students may never have eaten an all-American chocolate chip cookie. Contact the dean of students at the college to see if your church can provide cookies for international students when they first arrive at the college. He will direct you to an administrative staff person who can tell you how many international students will be living in the dormitories. When the students arrive at their dormitories, have a bag of American cookies waiting. Or, you may want to ask for permission for your church to provide cookies for their first orientation or meeting.

Consider a cookie ministry to international students during the Christmas holidays. Most of these students will have nowhere to go for the holidays. Turn this into a churchwide project. Ask women and men to provide cookies. Arrange with your minister of youth for the youth to visit the campus, sing Christmas carols, and distribute cookies to the international students. The children's department can decorate small plastic storage bags with Christmas stickers. The senior adults can provide Christmas cards. Remember to follow the rules and never to leave religious tracts or scripture portions without prior permission.

Jails
Do you live in a large city or a small town? Wherever you live, there is usually a jail nearby. These inmates need to know someone cares for them. Call the jail and ask for the chaplain or volunteer coordinator. Tell him about your cookie ministry and how your group could provide cookies for the inmates. Ask for permission to give cookies during

the Christmas season. A cookie ministry may open a door for the men in your church to begin a ministry, visiting and leading Bible studies. If your church is already involved in a prison outreach, you can expand it by providing cookies for the inmates.

Church members may also want to ask for permission to present an inspirational program or sing Christmas carols at the jail during the Christmas holidays. A Sunday School class or women's ministry group may make small bags of about six cookies each and a Christmas card for each inmate. Or, you may choose to deliver large trays of cookies instead. Consider covering shallow cardboard boxes that canned soft drinks come in with colorful Christmas wrapping paper. These bright holiday boxes will help add to the Christmas spirit for the inmates.

The jail's chaplain may suggest a time for you to provide cookies and soft drinks or punch to go with the cookies. Consider making this a churchwide project. The inmates will learn that someone cares for them. This is a good project for a small town with a small jail. The women in the church can bake the cookies, and the men can provide the soft drinks or punch and deliver the cookies to the inmates.

If you are in a large city where the jail houses several hundred inmates, consider suggesting this as a coordinating ministry for several churches. Each church can provide cookies and help serve the cookies to the inmates. Contact ministers in other churches in your city about joining in this ministry. You will need many cookies for a large jail with hundreds of inmates.

Transitional Families
Some churches provide temporary housing for individuals or families. Many times these individuals or families are unemployed and have financial problems and cannot afford to make rent payments. They need support and encouragement from others. They need to know that someone loves and cares for them. You can give them cookies and love. Contact the person in charge of the housing ministry at your church to find out when new residents will be moving in. Welcome the new residents with a visit and homemade cookies.

Consider enlisting a women's Sunday School class to bake cookies for these transitional families. Then visit the family during your church's regular visitation time. Women might also want to make decorative containers to hold the cookies. If they decorate coffee cans or gallon-sized glass jars with wide-mouth openings with contact paper, fabric, or bright stickers, the cookie jars will make a nice gift, too.

Look at all the possibilities for enlisting volunteers to bake cookies and/or make decorative containers for these cookies. This could be a project for a women's ministry group, the children's department, or a group of teenagers. What about the women and men in the church who enjoy making crafts? Your cookie ministry will grow as you enlist people to help with these fun projects.

Port Ministry
If you live on the coast in a port city, you can share cookies with the seafarers whose international ships dock in your city. Ask your pastor if there is already some sort of ministry to the sailors. Missionaries are sometimes assigned to lead port ministries. If there is a missionary in your area, tell him how your cookie ministry works, and ask if your church can provide cookies for the seafarers. If there is no missionary, find the administrative director of the dock and discuss your ministry with him.

Ask the missionary or appropriate administrative person about his work with the seafarers and how you can help. When appropriate, invite the missionary or administrator to speak to your church or organization about the international seafarers who dock their ships in your city. A guest speaker like this can get people excited about helping with the cookie ministry.

This is a good project for Christmas. Your churchwide ministry can provide cookies for these men and women who are hundreds of miles away from their families. The missionary or administrator can tell you how many people are on a ship at a given time. Enlist women and men to provide individual bags of cookies for each seaman. Place these bags in a large box covered in a bright Christmas gift wrap. Include a Christmas card with the name of your church. Even though they may not read English, they will enjoy the Christmas picture on the card. You are responsible for getting the cookies to the dock so the missionary or administrator can distribute the cookies.

This can be an opportunity for the men of your church to get involved. Consider asking a group of men to take the cookies to the dock. Although many of the seafarers will not speak English, they will know that people care for them. If you have someone in your church who speaks a foreign language, perhaps this can be the beginning of a new ministry for them.

Nursing Homes
Most towns have a local nursing home and larger cities usually have several nursing homes. Many of the residents do not have families nearby, and they become lonely and wish for someone to visit them.

Contact the activities' director of a nursing home, and tell her about your cookie ministry. Select a nursing home near your church or one where elderly church members reside.

You may choose a small nursing home, so you can give all the residents individual bags of cookies. Have four or five cookies in small, resealable plastic bags, and go into each room handing out cookies. Some residents are on special diets. The director will tell you which residents are not allowed to eat cookies. Provide fruit for these residents. Never give cookies to anyone who should not have them. If they ask you for one, tell them you must follow the rules. This ministry gives you a lot of personal contact with the residents as you visit the people and give them cookies. If you can do this on a monthly basis, the residents will come to look forward to your visits.

Consider this for a churchwide cookie ministry project. Enlist people to bake cookies and people to deliver them. If someone in the church leads Bible studies in the nursing home, ask if they would like to take the cookies for refreshments after the Bible study. Place cookies on brightly colored paper plates for this kind of event.

If your church is small, consider providing cookies for monthly birthday parties at the nursing home. Some residents do not attend the parties, so you will not need as many cookies. You might like to serve cookies at the party or enlist several church members to help you. A cookie ministry for birthday parties at a nursing home is idea for a small church in a little town.

Many nursing homes have a beverage cart to deliver milk, coffee, juice, or tea to the residents between meals. Ask about providing cookies to go with these beverages. Place the cookies in a large container or bag so that it will be easy to include on the beverage cart with the drinks. The person delivering the beverages will give cookies to the residents, your group will not need to visit in this case.

If your church is small and the nursing home that you choose has many residents, you can still have a cookie ministry. Consider providing cookies for the people who work at the nursing home. These workers have stressful days and will appreciate the cookies. The supervisor will tell you how many cookies to provide. Arrange the cookies on a paper plate or throw-away pie plates, and cover them with plastic wrap. If someone in the church works at the nursing home, they may want to take the cookies to the nursing home for the nurses and staff.

Home for Disabled People
Many times people with physical and/or mental disabilities require special care in a facility with trained staff. There are homes for disabled children and others for disabled adults. Physically and mentally disabled people live in these homes year-round.

Check your telephone book for the Association for Retarded Citizens or a school for disabled people. The administrative staff of these organizations can give you information about homes for disabled people in your local area. When you get this information, contact the social worker or administrative director of the home. Explain your cookie ministry, and ask if you can provide cookies for the residents at the home. These homes usually welcome visitors; however, always follow the rules. Consider taking cookies for the residents on special holidays. The administrator may prefer for you to bring the cookies and allow the staff to distribute them to the residents.

This is a good ministry for both large and small churches. Large churches can divide the responsibilities for baking, packaging, and delivering the cookies. Small churches can consider making individual cookie bags for the residents on special occasions.

Military Personnel
Do you have a military base near you? If so, consider a cookie ministry for service personnel stationed there. Contact the public relations department at the base and ask for permission to provide cookies for the personnel. They can tell you how many people they have stationed on base. Your churchwide cookie ministry may choose to provide cookies for the single men living in the barracks, baking cookies for a different barracks each month. You are responsible for enlisting someone to take the cookies to the base.

If you have base personnel in your church, ask if they will take the cookies to the base. This is a good ministry for the men and women of the church. The youth might also enjoy participating in this ministry. Each month teenagers could sign up to provide cookies and deliver them to the base. Then, if youth are interested, contact the base to see if the teenagers can deliver the cookies and tour the base.

This is a good project for a large church in a small town. It can be a monthly or seasonal ministry. The military personnel will enjoy cookies any time of the year. This is an ideal ministry for several churches who want to work together. Each month a different church could provide cookies for these men.

Children's Home
Children's homes provide house parents and a homelike atmosphere for children in transitional stages of their lives. These children attend churches, schools, and extra curricular activities just like other children. Ask your pastor if there is a children's

home in your town. If there is, contact the administrator or the house parents at the home and explain your cookie ministry. Ask if your church can provide cookies for the children living there. The administrator or house parents can tell you how many cookies they need for the children and arrange a time and place for delivery.

Consider this for a churchwide project. Enlist people to provide cookies and others to visit the children and distribute the cookies. You may want to provide juice or soft drinks to go with the cookies. Saturday is a good time for this kind of activity. A large church may want to consider this as a monthly ministry. You can provide cookies each month for a birthday party. The administrator or the house parents may prefer for you to bring the cookies and allow them to distribute the treats to the children. They may want to use the homemade cookies for the children's school lunch boxes.

Ronald McDonald House

Usually Ronald McDonald Houses are located in large cities near children's hospitals. Families from out of town stay in these homes to be near their sick child. People staying in these houses are experiencing a crisis and are often many miles away from their families. You can give cookies and love to people staying in a Ronald McDonald House if there is one located near you. Contact the manager of the house, and explain your cookie ministry. Ask if your church can provide cookies for these families.

You could take this on as a churchwide project. Consider making cookie jars or tins that can be kept in the kitchen and reused. Each time your church provides cookies, the family will have a cookie jar ready to store them. Paint a cheerful kitchen design on a wide-mouth glass jar (gallon sized) or decorate a cookie tin for this purpose.

As you visit these families you may learn of other needs they may have. Invite the families to your church and assure them that you will put their names on the church's prayerlist. Do not be pushy about religion and do not leave religious tracts without permission from the manager.

This is a good ministry for individuals or groups. Consider baking cookies each month or for special occasions. Before baking cookies, check with the manager to find out how many people are currently at the house.

Homeless Shelter

Many large cities have homeless shelters where men and women go for food and a place to sleep. Different organizations such as the Waterfront Rescue Mission or Salvation Army sponsor homeless shelters. Some shelters are sponsored by the combined efforts of local churches and their denominations. Look in your telephone book to see if a homeless shelter is in your area.

Contact the director of the shelter and explain your cookie ministry. Ask if you can provide cookies for the homeless. Make assignments within your church for delivering cookies to the shelter. You may want to ask someone who passes by the shelter on their way to work to deliver the cookies for you.

This can be an individual or group ministry. You may want to involve the men of the church in this ministry. Consider asking the women to provide the cookies and the men to deliver them. While they are at the shelter, the men may want to take time to visit with the homeless. One or two of the men might consider leading a Bible study at the shelter.

Women's Shelter

Many cities have shelters or homes for women and children who are victims of abuse. You may also have a women's rehabilitation home in your city for women who have abused alcohol or drugs. Women and children living in these kinds of shelters face stressful days and usually need assurance that people love and care for them. You can give cookies and love to these women and children.

Contact the director a women's shelter in your city, and explain your cookie ministry. Ask if your church can provide cookies for these women and children. Consider enlisting a Sunday School class or women's group to begin a cookie ministry to the women's shelter. Be sure to include a card from your church. These women and children need your church's love and attention.

Drug and Alcohol Rehabilitation Centers

Residents of drug and alcohol rehabilitation centers are faced with difficult and stressful days. They need love, concern, support, and encouragement from others. You can help provide this support through your cookie ministry. Look in your telephone book or ask your pastor about rehabilitation centers in your city. Talk to the director of the center about your cookie ministry. If your plan is acceptable, ask how many cookies will be needed and the best time of day to bring them.

The center may want cookies for monthly birthday parties or celebrations when the residents have completed the program. You may want to consider this for a churchwide ministry. The men of the church might like to deliver the cookies and visit with the people at the center. One or two of the men might choose to begin a Bible study for the people at the rehabilitation center.

Community Survey

When your church surveys the community for unchurched people, consider sending home baked cookies along. Talk with your church staff about combining your cookie ministry with the community survey. As you knock on doors, give people a small bag of cookies and information about programs available at your church. If the person is interested, share Jesus with them and invite them to your church.

Many dozens of cookies are necessary for this ministry. Everyone in the church can be involved. Some can bake cookies while others package them. Everyone may not be able to go on the survey, but they can help in many ways. Place the cookies in plastic bags and attach a religious tract or a card with the name and telephone number of your church on the outside. Have these ready to go on the day of the community survey. Each group will need a basket or large bag to hold their cookies. You will reach many people and have many opportunities to share Jesus with this cookie ministry project.

Church Visitation

Does your church have a regular visitation program? Consider providing cookies for the visitors to give to families they visit. Contact your pastor or a church staff member about your cookie ministry. They can help you decide how many cookies are needed. Provide a dozen cookies for each family that will be visited. Include a card with your church's name and telephone number on it on the outside of the bag or box of cookies. If there are people in your church who cannot bake cookies or participate in visitation, they may want to help by providing plastic bags for the cookies. Make sure you have plenty of cookies for the families visited and a few extras for the church members to eat as they are driving home from their visits.

My Cookie Ministries

I have started and led cookie ministries in three different churches. Of course, each church was a different size and had a variety of members with a variety of gifts and talents. Each church presented special opportunities because of its location and size. The following pages give a brief description of how I led these ministries.

Pensacola, Florida
While attending East Brent Baptist Church, I took my cookie ministry to a hospital, college, several shelters and temporary homes, and several other locations. I was even able to share American cookies with many internationals through a local university and through a port ministry. Here are some of the ways I found to give cookies and love.

Sacred Heart Hospital
I led the cookie ministry project for families in the day-surgery waiting room. Several days before we were to deliver the cookies, I enlisted bakers and assigned an amount of cookies for each person. They brought their cookies to the church on Wednesday night. One of the church members is a nurse at Sacred Heart Hospital. She picked up the cookies and took them to the hospital on Thursday morning. We had packed the cookies in a cookie tin, and she placed the tin near the coffee pot. A small card with the name of our church was taped to the top of the cookie tin.

Pensacola Junior College
Students at the junior college in Pensacola looked forward to our monthly cookie day. I enlisted several women to bake cookies; enough for a large box each time. Then, everyone brought their homemade cookies to the church. One of the church members is a student ministries director at the college. He picked up the cookies and distributed them the next day. I discovered that chocolate chip cookies are the students' favorite.

Students at Pensacola Junior College have a central meeting place sponsored by Baptist student ministries. The building, across the street from the college campus, is open for all students without regard to religious affiliation. They use the building to study and hold various meetings and celebrations. We regularly provided cookies to be distributed at this meeting place.

University of West Florida
New international students received a welcome bags of cookies from my church. At the beginning of the spring term, several members of the church baked cookies and brought them to church. Other volunteers put cookies in small plastic bags and included a welcome-to-the-United-States card. A person who worked at the college picked up the cookies from the church.

Escambia County Jail
We provided cookies and a party during the Christmas holidays for the inmates at the county jail. Because there are several hundred inmates, I had to call on several area churches to help with this ministry. Several people from each church went to the jail to help serve at the party. The church members who worked on this project received a blessing, and the inmates enjoyed an evening of cookies, fellowship, and inspiration.

East Brent Baptist Church Temporary Housing
This house is located across the street from the church. The families or individuals who live here temporarily have financial problems and other stresses. Through the cookie ministry, we were able to lessen the stresses for a moment or two. Usually, two women visited the family and took cookies. We visited for a while, showed our love and concern, and gave them the cookies. We also scheduled a welcome shower each time new residents moved in. Cookies were a major part of the refreshments for this event.

Pensacola Port Ministry
International seafarers who docked in our area during the Christmas season received homemade

cookies from my church. Several women in the church volunteered to bake cookies. Since the port ministry missionary is a member of the church, he picked up the cookies from the church and delivered them to the men aboard ship.

Mobile, Alabama Children's Home
East Brent Baptist Church is near Mobile, Alabama. We were able to visit the children's home in Mobile occasionally. We would take cookies and soft drinks and join the children in an afternoon snack. Our visits with these children was such a rewarding experience that it remains a cherished memory for me.

Ronald McDonald House
My church's cookie ministry provided cookies every month for the families staying at the local Ronald McDonald House. Volunteers baked cookies and brought them to the church. Other volunteers met the next day and packed the cookies for each family at the home. Then two or three women took the cookies to the house. Many times the women would spend a little time visiting with the families. This was a successful project for us and the Ronald McDonald House. We received several requests for more cookies.

Waterfront Rescue Mission Homeless Shelter
The men at the homeless shelter enjoyed homemade cookies provided by my church every month. We always put the cookies in small plastic bags, so they would be convenient for the men to take with them. We also included a religious tract and a note of encouragement from our church for each day. Sometimes we decorated brown lunch bags and put the cookies and tracts inside. My husband got involved in this ministry by volunteering to deliver the cookies to the shelter on his way to work.

New Hope Home
This home is a drug and alcohol rehabilitation center sponsored by the Waterfront Rescue Mission in Pensacola. They hold a graduation ceremony when the residents complete a three-month residential program. Our cookie ministry provided cookies for the receptions following the ceremonies. I enlisted bakers to make cookies and bring them to the church. Then, several other volunteers put the cookies in small plastic bags. We included a religious tract and a note of encouragement from our church. My husband took the cookies to the center in time for the ceremonies.

Waterfront Rescue Mission Woman's Shelter
This shelter provides women and children with support and encouragement that they desperately need. We were able to be a part of this ministry by providing cookies and love. We delivered the cookies in pretty decorative baskets to add a little cheer. (Directions for making these baskets are in the chapter titled Cookie Carriers.) My husband took these cookies to the Waterfront Rescue Mission, and their staff delivered them to the shelter for the women and children.

East Brent Baptist Church Community Survey
Our church had a Super Saturday event where members went into the community inviting people to church. They gave out bags of cookies to each home they visited. I enlisted everyone in the church to bake cookies. They brought the cookies to the church on Friday, and volunteers put them in small plastic bags. Each bag included a tract and information about the church. On Saturday morning, the cookies were all packed and ready to go.

Church Visitation
When visitors come to East Brent Baptist Church, a team of church members go to their home to visit and invite them back to our church. Each team takes along a bag of cookies. For this cookie ministry project, a group of women come to the church and bake the cookies. They also put the cookies in individual bags with a printed message that says, Baked with Love.

I focus my cookie ministry on unchurched people in the community. So, the visitation program at East Brent is not a part of my responsibilities. However, it is a ministry of my church, and I wanted to let you know about it. You will need to set the guidelines for your cookie ministry.

Destin, Florida
While attending Village Baptist Church, I was able to give cookies and love to disabled people and the elderly.

Fort Walton Beach Developmental Center
Several teenagers visited and provided refreshments at this home for mentally disabled children and adults. The youth baked cookies and made punch for the residents, then spent an afternoon at the center with the residents. The teenagers and the residents enjoyed their time together.

Nursing Home
A group of women in the church visited the local nursing every month. We gave individual bags of cookies to the residents. One church member who baked cookies was 90 years old; older than most of the nursing home residents!

Fort Walton Beach, Florida
While attending Cinco Baptist Church in Fort Walton Beach, I had the special opportunity of leading a cookie ministry to provide cookies for sailors at the local coast guard station.

Fort Walton Beach Coast Guard Station
A group of teenagers in the church came to my house and baked cookies. We would do this on an afternoon after school or on a Saturday. When we had all the cookies baked and packaged, the teenagers and I would go to the coast guard station and deliver the cookies to the sailors. The men appreciated the cookies and always offer us a tour of the station.

More Ministries
♥♥♥♥♥

These additional ministries may be available in your city or a town near your home. I hope you can participate in some of these areas of ministries. Organizations and groups that are available in one area may not be available in another area. However, wherever you live, you can look for opportunities to brighten someone's day with cookies.

Seasonal Tourists

Resort towns attract seasonal visitors. I live in Florida where we have many retirees come to to live during the winter months. They enjoy the comfortable, warm weather and participate in many of our community events. Some of these tourists travel in recreational vehicles, motor homes, or campers. They stay at private, county, or state operated campgrounds or travel parks.

Florida is not the only state that attracts seasonal tourists. Is there a campground in your town? If so, contact the campground manager and tell him about your cookie ministry. Ask if you church can provide cookies for these winter tourists. You may also want to ask for permission to give tracts or scripture portion with the cookies. The manger cannot tell you the exact numbers of campers at a given time, but he can tell you the number of campsites available. He will also know the approximate number of campers he expects during the Christmas holidays. Because of the number of campers will be unpredictable, take along extra bags of cookies whenever you go.

Small churches in a small towns may choose to participate in a once-a-year activity to go Christmas caroling and give out cookies to the campers. Encourage everyone in the church to be involved. With lots of promotion and publicity, this can be a tremendous activity for your church. The women of the church can bake large recipes of cookies. Groups of children and teenagers can decorate boxes, plastic bags, containers, or baskets with paint, Christmas wrapping paper, or pictures of cookies. Other volunteers can sort the cookies in groups of 12 and pack them in the containers.

On the day of the cookies and caroling ministry, everyone should meet at the church. Each group of no more than ten people need to have a large basket or plastic grocery bag with handles to carry the smaller containers of cookies. Remember to have plenty of religious tracts or church bulletins to give the campers if this is permitted by the campground manager. When everyone gets to the campground, each group should go in a different direction, caroling and passing out cookies as they circulate through the campground.

Consider making Christmas cards for the campers, too. You can use a computer with a greeting card program and make copies of the card. Or, you can use boxed Christmas cards and stamp or write the name of your church on the inside.

This cookie ministry can be a fun annual event for your church and for the campers. Many campers are hundreds of miles from their families during this time and will appreciate the cookies and love that your church can give. Offer an invitation to the campers to visit your church.

Fair Workers

Most communities have a county fair each year and some big cities sponsor a big state fair. This is often a festive time, attracting many people whether it is held in a small town or a large city. Someone at your city hall or county courthouse can give you a telephone number for the fair promoters. Contact the director of this event and explain your cookie ministry. Ask if your church can provide cookies to the fair workers. Ask for permission to give cookies and tracts to the workers. These workers often travel from town to town with the fair, spending many days on the road traveling and away from their families. You can give cookies and love to these workers.

This is an ideal ministry for a church in a small town. The women and men in the church can provide cookies while the children and youth make containers and package them. One or two people can take the cookies to the fairgrounds or to the administrative office of the fair promoters. If you have permission to give tracts, place them with the box of cookies. Consider making this an annual ministry project. The workers will look forward to coming to your town. They will know that they will receive a warm welcome.

Support Groups
Some churches offer support groups for various needs. Single parents, adults who come from dysfunctional families, and people who are the principal caregivers of family members with illnesses such as Parkinson, Alzheimer, or cancer, are only a few of the areas of support that may be offered by your church. Contact the group leaders, and tell them about your cookie ministry. Ask them if you can provide cookies for their group meetings on a regular basis or for special occasions. The leader can tell you how many, when, and where to bring cookies.

Are there other kinds of support groups available in your community? Look in your newspaper and telephone book to see what groups are available in your area. Contact the Salvation Army or a local hospital about support groups that they offer. People in support groups need encouragement and to know that someone in the community cares about them. Decide which group or groups your church would like to help. Enlist someone to take the cookies to the meeting. If the group meeting is not confidential, they may allow you to sit in on their meeting when you deliver the cookies. You may learn about other needs of the people. The support group may want someone from your church to share a devotion at the meeting. If appropriate, assure the group that you will place them on the church's prayerlist.

Bus Travelers
Most cities have a bus station. Traveling by bus is the only means of travel for many people because it is less expensive than flying. Senior adults who do not drive often use buses to visit their families. Young military men often travel across country and spend several days on buses and in bus stations. These travelers may spend an hour or more sitting in a waiting area for their next bus. Visit the bus station, and tell the manager about your cookie ministry. Ask if your church can provide cookies to these tired and weary travelers. If you can obtain permission, place individually wrapped cookies in a cookie tin or box near the ticket desk. Tape a small card with the name and telephone number of your church on the tin or box. Travelers who do not have extra money for snacks will especially enjoy the cookies. Consider taking the cookies to the bus station in the afternoon so tired and weary travelers can enjoy the cookies while waiting through the night. This can be a monthly ministry or one just for special holidays.

Summertime Bible Schools and Clubs
Summer missionaries and church youth groups often travel to other areas and lead in these week-long activities for children. These events can be held in someone's yard or carport, a school yard, park, or the community meeting area of an apartment complex. Most of these events are small and will probably have less than 20 children attending each day. The children listen to Bible stories, memorize Bible verses, play games, and sing songs. And if they are recipients of your cookie ministry, they eat home baked cookies.

Enlist three or four women to bake six dozen cookies each. Hershey Great American Chocolate Chip Cookie recipe makes six dozen cookies and the recipe is found in the chapter titled Favorite Recipes. Assign each person a particular day to bake cookies. Or, you may choose to have ten women (two per day) bake three dozen cookies each. Either way, you will have plenty of cookies for the children and the workers. You are responsible for taking the cookies to the meeting site each day.

Agricultural Migrants
Farmers who move from state to state to pick fruits and vegetables in season are called migrants. They usually travel with their families and work long hours for low wages. Sometimes the children work in the fields to help earn money for the family. Churches have opportunities to minister to these migrant farmers while they are working in the community. If you live in an area where migrants come to harvest the crops, consider giving them cookies and love. You may want to include all the area churches in this ministry.

Ask the local farmer who has contracted for migrant workers when he expects the migrants to arrive. Tell him about your cookie ministry and ask for permission to provide cookies for the migrant families. Also, ask for permission to include religious tracts or scripture portions with the cookies. He can tell you how many families he expects and the approximate dates for their arrival. If this will be a multi-church ministry, planning before the migrants arrive will make this ministry go smoother. Proper planning will give all the churches the necessary information about this ministry.

Each church should be responsible for delivering three dozen cookies in quart-sized plastic bags to the farm at an agreed upon time. Some churches may want to include containers of presweetened soft drink mix with their cookies. Church members should plan on giving out the cookies and drink mix at a time and in a manner that will not interrupt the farmers' work.

Teenagers often enjoy helping with this kind of

ministry. They can plan programs and activities for the migrant children. Some can dress up as clowns to pass out cookies while others present puppet shows and/or storytellings.

Soup Kitchens

Some cities have soup kitchens to provide meals for people who are hungry. Churches and Christian organizations usually sponsor these kitchens. Ask your pastor about the soup kitchens in your city. You may find a soup kitchen listed in your telephone book under Social Service Organizations. If there is a soup kitchen in your community, contact the director, and explain your cookie ministry. Ask for if your church can provide cookies to go with the lunches. Arrange a day and time to deliver the cookies. The director will tell you how many cookies they need at any given time. Consider this for a monthly ministry or just for special holidays. Whichever you choose, the hungry men and women will enjoy your cookies.

Angel Tree

Some churches have an Angel Tree in their foyer during the Christmas season. Angel Tree is a ministry of Prison Fellowship. For more information, write: Angel Tree, A Ministry of Prison Fellowship National Office, P. O. Box 17500, Washington, DC 20041-0500. Each construction-paper angel on the tree has written on it a wish and the name of a child who has a parent in prison. Each child will have two angels on the tree. One wish will be for clothing and the other wish will be for a toy. Individuals, families, or groups choose an angel from the tree and purchase gifts for the child.

Cookies can be an extra special treat for the children. The cookie ministry can provide cookies for each family of children on the angel tree. People who cannot afford to buy gifts can help by giving cookies. More people in the church can be involved in an existing ministry. The leader of the cookie ministry and the chairperson of the Angel Tree ministry should work together. The chairperson of an Angel Tree ministry can tell you how many children are represented and how many cookies will be needed. The person baking cookies may choose to add a special touch to the cookies by using Christmas cookie cutters or decorate them with colorful frosting. A Sunday School class may help by making decorated bags or baskets for the cookies.

Agree upon the best time to take the cookies and gifts to the families. With careful planning and everyone working together, this can be a special time for everyone involved in this ministry.

Make a Difference Day

The last Saturday of October is Make a Difference Day. Your church can make a difference by giving cookies to others. Have a cookie giveaway (instead of a bake sale). Make posters to promote your cookie giveaway. Place them on community bulletin boards and in the yard near the entrance of your church. Set up tables outside your church and give cookies to people who come by. You can wrap cookies individually or place several in small plastic bags. Hand out tracts and information about your church at this time, too.

For information about Make a Difference Day call 1-800-416-3824, or write: USA Weekend Make a Difference Day, 1000 Wilson Boulevard, Arlington VA 22229-0012.

How to Begin a Cookie Ministry

Do you want to be a leader of a team that will bring joy to others? Is God calling you for a cookie ministry? If the answer is yes, ask God where He wants you to begin. After reading the many opportunities of service in this book, you are ready to begin a cookie ministry. However, there are many steps to follow; the same as in baking cookies. If you have the correct ingredients and follow the recipe, you will have good cookies. This principle also applies to following the necessary procedures for an effective cookie ministry. The effectiveness of your ministry will reflect the degree of your commitment to carry out the responsibilities required of the leadership position.

Give a copy of *Giving Cookies and Love* to your pastor, minister of education, and senior adult minister. Tell them about your ideas for the cookie ministry and the kind of project that you want to begin in your church. You must have all your plans and facts together before you present it to them. Ask for their suggestions and help in beginning and leading this ministry. Their support and prayers are essential for a successful ministry in your church. If your church already has an outreach ministry, you can work together to make cookies an addition to the existing ministry. Do the ministries that everyone can agree on. To be effective a cookie ministry must be a joint effort. Remember to pray and ask for God's guidance in beginning and leading this new ministry in your church.

Responsibilities

Responsibility go along with receiving blessings. Your first decision will be which group to give cookies to. If your church has an ongoing ministry, consider adding cookies to it. You will be responsible for obtaining permission from the appropriate authority for your church to provide cookies to an organization or group. Then, you will need to enlist volunteers to bake cookies. The responsibility for delivering the cookies lies with you. You may enlist someone to take the cookies, or you may want to accept that duty yourself. Most importantly, you need to be flexible. You must like to bake cookies and be able to bake them on short notice when others cannot.

These responsibilities are essential for a church-wide ministry. This is a ministry that the whole church can participate in. There is a job for everyone who is interested. If you and your church staff agree on having a cookie ministry as a small group project, you, as the leader, will have the same responsibilities. Whichever ministry you choose, you will always be able to find people willing to bake cookies to give to others.

Choosing a Ministry

Begin your cookie ministry with one monthly project. Plan to deliver the cookies the same time each month such as the first Monday or second Thursday. This is easier for everyone to keep track of when to bake cookies and when to expect cookies to be delivered. Do you have a special place in your heart for people in a nursing home or college students? You may choose an organization or group that is convenient to you or your church, maybe a hospital or a children's home. Stay with one ministry for a year before you add others. You will gain confidence and become willing to take on more responsibility.

Small churches may want to provide cookies on special occasions to different groups. For example, when the local fair comes to town once a year, your church can welcome the workers with cookies. At Christmas you can provide cookies for the inmates at the local jail or residents in a nursing home. Your first step is to decide the recipients of your cookie ministry. Pray about this decision, and ask God where He wants you to begin your ministry. When you feel comfortable about your decision, you are ready to contact the person in charge of the organization.

Call the organization or group and make an appointment to visit the director. Consider providing a written plan of your cookie ministry proposal. In some cases a telephone call will be sufficient for approval to begin a ministry. However, it is best to meet the people you will be working with before you deliver cookies. Be sure to have all the necessary information about your ministry so that you can share your project with enthusiasm. Let the director see that you are a loving and caring person and that you are genuine in your desire to help others. Be prepared to answer questions and allow the director time to discuss the plan with the employees. Do not get discouraged. This may take several phone calls or visits before you receive approval.

Once you receive permission, the director can tell you how many people to provide cookies for. The two of you should also agree on the time and place for the cookies to be delivered. Be sure to enlist someone who is reliable to deliver the cookies whenever the organization or group wants them. In some cases, you may want to take on this responsibility yourself. In some cases, groups of church members will want to deliver the cookies and visit with the people who will be receiving the cookies. Now that you have selected a place for your cookie ministry, and you have received permission to provide them with cookies, your next responsibility is to enlist bakers.

Publicity

Now that you have chosen your ministry and have secured approval to begin, you need cookies, and you must enlist volunteers to bake them. Make sure everyone knows who will be the recipients of the cookies. When people know who will receive the cookies, they are usually eager to help. Don't begin your ministry by saying we are going to bake cookies without having someone selected to give them to. People don't often want to spent time baking cookies if they don't know why they are baking them.

You need publicity to let everyone know about the new cookie ministry and that you need people to bake cookies. Your enthusiasm will go a long way in getting people to volunteer. Get the information out to everyone about what is going on in your church.

You may want to do your publicity in several different ways. Plan a big promotion of the cookie ministry once a year, but enlist interested people throughout the year. If your church has a time to make announcements at the beginning of worship service, ask the pastor (or whoever makes announcements) to announcement the beginning of a new cookie ministry. Write what you want him to say neatly and legibly on a piece of paper, and give it to him several days before the service. Make sure all the necessary information is on the announcement.

Share your enthusiasm with your pastor, church staff, and church family. If you are in a small church, you may have several opportunities to make the announcement yourself. Be very enthusiastic about what you are saying. In other words, sell your product to the congregation. A sample announcement is in the chapter titled Samples and Announcements. Contact the Minister of Education or Sunday School director for permission to make announcements in Sunday School classes. If there are several classes, plan to go to a different class each Sunday.

Have a sign-up sheet ready for volunteers to sign up to bake cookies. Ask for their name, telephone number, and when they want to bake cookies; monthly or quarterly. I have included a sample sign up list in the chapter titled Samples and Announcements.

Consider publicizing the cookie ministry in your church newsletter. This way, everyone who is a member of the church should have an opportunity to learn about the new cookie ministry. Place the information in the newsletter during the same week or two that you are promoting your ministry in church and Sunday School. Write out your announcement, and give it to your church secretary. Be sure to include all the necessary information, including your name and telephone number, so people can contact you if they want to be a part of the ministry. A sample announcement is in the chapter titled Samples and Announcements.

Get permission to publicize your ministry on church bulletin boards. Use brightly colored paper to make posters. Use bold marking pens to trace stencils or draw freehand large letters to spell out Cookie Ministry. Decorate your poster with pictures of cookies cut from magazines. Add a sign-up list to the bottom of the poster. Be sure to include all the necessary information, including your name and telephone number for others to contact you. Make your poster neat, attractive, and eye appealing. A bright attractive poster will capture the attention of people passing by.

Another good way to promote the cookie ministry is to have a guest speaker from the organization that you will be providing cookies for to speak at your church. This, of course, must be coordinated with your pastor for a scheduled date and time. Plan several weeks ahead for this publicity. Ask the guest speaker to tell about the people who will receive the cookies and other ways you can help in this organization. The pastor may want to have a guest speaker come to the church when he is out of town. As the leader of the cookie ministry, you will introduce the guest speaker and make an announcement about the need to bake cookies for this group. Have a sign-up sheet on a table in the foyer so people can sign up to bake cookies. Plan to be at the table available to answer questions, after your guest speaks.

Keep copies of the announcements that were read to the congregation and Sunday School classes and a copy of the announcement placed in the church newsletter in a notebook for future use. Use another notebook to file the sign-up sheets. Each month as people bake cookies, write the date by their name. A computer will be helpful in keeping track of your publicity announcements and in keeping up with your cookie ministry volunteers.

Now that you have your place of ministry and volunteers to bake cookies, you need to decide what day for the volunteers to bake cookies and when and where they should put them.

Cookie Day

Sunday is a good day to bring cookies to church. If your church has a midweek service, consider asking volunteers to bring their cookies to the church on that day. When people are already going to be a church anyway, try to make it convenient for them to bring their cookies then, too. It is best to choose the same day every month, and let it become routine. You can deliver the cookies on the same day or the following day.

Your next decision is where to put the cookies. The church office, kitchen, and fellowship hall are good locations. Everyone usually knows where to find these rooms. You choose a location that is best for your church. Now that you have a day and a designated room, you need a box to hold the cookies.

Cookie Box

Make a large cookie box to hold the bags of cookies. Cardboard boxes that photocopy paper comes in are great for this purpose. If you have only one ministry, use the same box each month. When you add to your ministries, getting a new box each time may be easier for you. Place the cookie box in its designated room well before people begin to arrive at the church.

Put a sign on the box that says Cookie Ministry. A sample sign is in the chapter titled Samples and Announcements. Consider cutting brightly colored poster board to fit one end of the box. Then, staple it to the front end. Decorate the box with pictures of cookies cut from magazines. Be creative and neat in decorating your box. Allow enough room for a half-page of white paper; the list of names of the people who baked cookies. A reproducible sample is in the chapter titled Samples and Announcements. Have the bakers check off their name when they bring their cookies.

Instead of a cardboard box, you may choose to purchase a plastic storage container for your cookie box. Mine is 15-by-21-by-12 and has a hinged top. These containers are often sold in discount stores. My husband placed 3-inch stick-on letters on the lid of the box to spell out Cookies. I have two grocery bags in the bottom of the box to hold the bags of cookies. When all the cookies are delivered to the church and packaged as appropriate, I place the containers into the grocery bags. They are then ready for delivery.

Cookie Letters

Now you have completed all the steps to begin your cookie ministry. It looks as if everything is in order and you are ready to begin. You have decided your place of ministry such as a hospital. You have approval from the manager to begin your ministry. The volunteers are ready to bake cookies. You have decided when they will bring their cookies to church. Also, you have selected the room where you will put the cookie box. Now you are ready to get your letters ready to send to the women who will be baking cookies. A computer or typewriter will be an asset when you prepare these letters. If either of these is not available, make sure your handwriting is neat and legible.

Include all necessary information in your letters. Always begin your letter by thanking the person for being a part of the cookie ministry. Tell them who will receive the cookies. They will need to know many cookies to bake and when and where to bring them. A sample of what to include in your letter is in the chapter titled Samples and Announcements.

Give the church secretary a copy of your letter and a list of the people to send the letter to. She will have the addresses. Ask her to make copies of the letter and mail them to the volunteers who are to bake cookies. Volunteers need to receive their letters several days before you need the cookies. So, allow the church secretary ample time to copy and mail the letters. Do not give her the letter one day and expect her to mail them the next. Thank her for sending out the letters; and remember her during secretary's week!

You can calculate the number of cookies you need by allowing four to six cookies per person in the group. (For example, if there 12 students at the children's home, multiply 12 by 4 or 6. You will need at least 48 or 72 cookies.) The number of cookies you need will determine the number of volunteer bakers you need to enlist, and therefore, the number of letters that you will need to send out. If these are for a hospital waiting room, it is difficult to know how many you will need. Consider asking bakers to bake their favorite recipe of cookies. Most recipes make at least three dozen. Always ask at least one or two extra people to bake cookies. From experience, I can tell you that there will always be someone who forgets to bake cookies and does not call you.

Cookie Calls

If you or your church would prefer not to spend money on postage, call the volunteers. These can be your Cookie Calls. Always be very enthusiastic in your conversation about the cookie ministry. Have in front of you a copy of a letter with all the necessary information on it when you make each call. Tell who will receive the cookies, how many to bake, when and where to bring cookies. Always give your telephone number, so the bakers can call you if they have any questions. Thank them for being a part of the ministry. Remember to make your calls several days before you need the cookies.

Be as persistent as necessary, and talk directly to the volunteer baker. Do not leave the message; on an answering machine or with another person. Just leave your name and telephone number and ask the person to return your call.

Ministry in Action

Now you are ready to begin your ministry. You have selected an organization or group to receive your cookies, and you have obtained permission from the appropriate authorities to begin your ministry. You have your list of volunteers willing to bake cookies. The church secretary has sent them a letter, giving them all the information about bringing their cookies to church. (If you choose to call the volunteers, then you will need to give them all the information about when and where to bring the cookies.) Now everyone will know where to take the cookies. The cookie box should be in the room ready for early arrivals. Now you are responsible for getting the cookies to the selected place of ministry.

As you can see, there are many steps involved before you can begin your ministry. Follow each step in the correct order. This is the same as adding ingredients to a cookie recipe. All steps are essential for an effective ministry.

Always call to remind the director or administrator of the organization that you will be bringing cookies. And, be sure to deliver the cookies on the scheduled time and day. If you plan to package the cookies in individual bags, you will need someone to help you. Another group of volunteers can help with this stage of the project. Remember to enclose a small card with the name and telephone number of your church. If you have obtained permission to include religious tracts, do this also. Some places do not allow you to leave religious tracts or literature, so do not do this unless you have already obtained permission. Always remember to follow the rules. Your church is a silent witness to the employees and the ones receiving the cookies.

Delivering cookies is a special event. Always remember to smile and let the love of the Lord show through you. You represent Jesus and your church in your community.

May God bless you as you begin your new and unique ministry. You will receive many blessings along the way. You may also have some discouraging days such as when people forget to bake cookies. Do not give up. Keep on trying. Remember the reasons you are involved in the ministry. You bake and give the cookies with love because you and others love Jesus.

Individual Ministries
♥♥♥♥

You can begin a ministry in your own neighborhood. There are many ministries projects right outside your front door. Look around you. Your neighbors, friends and co-workers need cookies and love. Most ministry projects will be twofold, you visit a person or group and give them cookies. As you minister, you will have opportunities to tell others about Jesus. No matter what kind of ministry project you choose, always let those with whom you work see Jesus in you in everything you do or say. You are a representative of Jesus and your church; represent them well. Let people see that you are genuine in your love and concern. Be available to these people in their time of need. You may not be able to solve their problems, but you can always pray for them and do what you can.

You do not have to have an occasion to give cookies. You can make any ordinary day more memorable with a gift of cookies. Surprise a friend or relative with a gift of cookies any time. Use your calendar as a reminder for baking and giving gifts. Holidays offer the perfect opportunity to give cookies and love. Use cookie cutters and presses, frosting and sprinkles to add a special touches.

Cookies will be even more delightful when delivered in attractive cookie carriers. Decorated bags, boxes, baskets, or jars always add a smile, and can be reused to hold more cookies or other items. Suggestions for making cookie carriers are found in the chapter titled Cookie Carriers. Always include an inspirational card with your cookies. Pocket-sized cards are inexpensive and can be purchased at Christian bookstores. You can make inspirational cards by writing uplifting Bible verses or putting religious stickers on index cards. This is your witness to others when you give cookies and love. There are many blessings waiting for you as you share with others.

New Neighbor
Do you often see a moving van in your neighborhood? New neighbors will appreciate a warm welcome. When someone moves into your neighborhood, visit them and give them cookies. Ask how you can help to make their move easier, and invite them to visit your church.

Offer them a church bulletin or newsletter, so they can learn about the programs of your church. Make your first visit brief, but promise to stop by another time and tell them about shopping, local activities, and community events in their new neighborhood.

Bereaved Family
Bereavement is a common and painful experience in our lives. Everyone will face the loss of family members and close friends. People especially need love and support during this difficult time. Show your love and concern to a bereaved family with a visit and a plate of homemade cookies. Ask the family if you can pray with them. If the family does not have a church, consider asking your church to provide a meal for them.

Homebound
Many senior adults cannot drive and get around like they did when they were younger. Some have painful arthritis and other health problems that keep them close to their home. Many have families who live several miles away. These senior adults become lonely and need love and care. Call senior adults in your neighborhood. Ask them if you can visit and bring some cookies. This is an ideal monthly ministry for an individual. The senior adults will look forward to your visits. You will be giving your time, love, and cookies.

If your church has a television ministry, share this with your homebound neighbors. Tell them the time and channel, so they can watch your church on television. Consider also sharing audio tapes from your church service if your homebound neighbor has a tape player.

All homebound people are not senior adults. People of all ages can be victims of accidents or serious diseases. They will also enjoy a visit and some homemade cookies from a neighbor. Always call and ask when will be a good time for a visit.

Families in Crisis
Do you have friends or neighbors facing difficult times in their lives? Perhaps they are facing a job loss, family problems, serious illness, or other stressful situations. Families need to know someone cares for them during these stressful days. Visit the family for a short visit and give them some homemade cookies. Just let them know that you care about them during this time. Do not question them about their situation; just tell them that you will be praying for them. If the family does not attend church, invite them to your church. Consider asking your pastor or a church elder to visit with this family.

Beauty Shops
Consider giving cookies and love to the beauticians and customers at a community beauty shop. Ask the manager of the shop for permission to provide cookies for the beauticians and customers. You probably will not have the opportunity to share Jesus in this business atmosphere, but you can be a silent witness. Your conservation and attitude will go a long way in telling people who you are. You may have the opportunity to share about an event in your church. Or, someone may ask why you baked cookies for them. When you are asked, tell them about your cookie ministry and your church.

Hospitalized Family Member
All of us, at one time or another, have had a family member in the hospital. Some hospital stays are brief while others are for long periods of time. This is very stressful, and often hectic, for all family members; the one in the hospital and the ones taking care of him. Family members often split their time between visiting at the hospital, working, and doing household chores. Usually the hospitalized person gets all the attention. However, the other family members need some extra attention also during this time. This is especially true of children.

   Bake a batch of cookies and take them to the family. Tell them that you will pray for them and will put their family on the prayerlist at your church. If their prayer request is printed in a bulletin or on a prayer sheet, give them a copy. Your ministry will be very meaningful to them during this time.

Baking Cookies at Church

Most churches have an outreach ministry to others in the community. Sometimes lay members lead Bible studies in nursing homes, jails, or homeless shelters for men or women. Who does your church reach out to in the community? A cookie ministry can be an addition to an existing ministry. This will open doors for women to serve by baking cookies.

Wives of church staff members can begin this cookie ministry to their community. The group will need a chairperson to lead the ministry. She should like to bake cookies and not work outside the home during the day. You will only need about four people to come to the church and bake cookies for this ministry. The volunteers will bake cookies on the morning of a night outreach ministry. (If the ministry is during the morning or afternoon, the bakers need to bake their cookies the day before the outreach.)

Have a sign-up list so the women can choose when they will come to the church and bake cookies. Some may want to come each week while others may want to volunteer only once a month. With a sign-up list, you will be able to keep a schedule of when everyone will bake cookies. If you decide to assign volunteers a particular month to bake cookies, you will need to send them a letter or call them with the necessary information.

The number of cookies the women will need to bake will depend on the number of people involved in the ministry. Work closely with the lay leader of the outreach ministry that you are going to supplement with cookies. Ask them how many cookies they will need, but always provide some extras. The outreach ministry may grow because people will come to eat cookies. The smell of a plate of fresh homemade cookies always attracts a crowd!

When you are baking cookies at the church, you need to decide how you will get the needed ingredients. Enlist someone to be responsible for ordering, purchasing, or collecting the necessary ingredients. She will make sure there are plenty of ingredients for each baking time. You may obtain the ingredients for the cookies in several ways. You may be able to add the cost of ingredients to the church budget, or you can ask church members to donate the necessary ingredients. Consider assigning individual ingredients to each Sunday School class. This way you will not have 20 bottles of vanilla extract and no brown sugar.

Promote your cookie ingredients donation drive a couple Sundays before you need the ingredients. This will give everyone time to buy their ingredients. A sample announcement is in the chapter titled Samples an Announcements. Place collection boxes in each Sunday School room. Include an envelope for money in case some people want to sponsor the purchase of eggs and butter.

Another option for acquiring the needed ingredients is for your church to take a special offering for the purchase of ingredients for the cookie pantry. As church members drop in small change, the money adds up for the ministry.

What works in one church may not be feasible in another. So, do whatever works best for your church. However you get your ingredients, set up a cookie pantry devoted solely to the cookie ministry. Eggs and butter should be kept in the refrigerator and the expiration dates monitored.

Now it looks like your ministry is moving right along. You have someone to lead the ministry and your church has decided how to get money for ingredients to bake cookies. Someone is responsible for purchasing or collecting ingredients. There is a schedule of when each person will come to the church and bake cookies. When the cookies have cooled, the women will package them in plastic bags or non-returnable containers. Now everything is ready for someone to take the cookies to the designated ministry. Whichever outreach ministry you choose, the recipients will know the cookies were baked and given with love.

Samples and Announcements
♥♥♥♥

You can use these announcements for church, Sunday School, church bulletin, newsletter, or bulletin boards. Complete the blanks to meet your individual needs for promoting the cookie ministry in your church. The sign-up list works well when placed on the bulletin board with the announcement. You may also circulate the sign-up list in the Sunday School classes. If you choose a different ministry, these announcement samples will help you in wording your announcement. You will find various samples to help you in your ministry. A card to include with your cookies will be essential in your ministry. You may copy these sample pages for church use only.

Cookie Ministry

Do you like to bake cookies?

Your help is needed to bake cookies for our cookie ministry.

We provide cookies monthly for
_____

Contact _____
at_____
to be a part of the cookie ministry.

Announcing:
Hospital Cookie Ministry

We will provide cookies for the families in the waiting room at

_____
Hospital.

We need you to help bake cookies.
Call the church office
_____
for more information.

Announcing:
Nursing Home Cookie Ministry

Our church is beginning a cookie ministry for the nursing home.

Join in this ministry by baking cookies.

_____

Sign-up List for Cookie Ministry

Name _____
Phone _____
Address _____

I will bake cookies
____ Monthly ____ Quarterly ____ Yearly

For information call _____
at _____

When you need to make cookie carriers post the following notice and show a completed carrier or two.

Needed:
Items to make cookie carriers for the cookie ministry.

Items needed:
- ribbon
- paper twist
- oat canisters
- lunch bags
- plastic sandwich bags
- greeting cards (used)
- yarn
- plastic strawberry baskets
- English muffin boxes
- plastic freezer bags
- gift wrap (new or used)

Cookie Ministry Box

Place your cookies in this box.
For more information on how to be a part of this ministry call
_____ at _____

Thanks for being a part of our cookie ministry.
Place a check by your name when you bring your cookies.

Name _____	Name _____
Name _____	Name _____
Name _____	Name _____
Name _____	Name _____
Name _____	Name _____
Name _____	Name _____

Cookie Letter
Write a personal letter to the people who volunteer to bake cookies. Include in your letter:
- a word of thanks for being a part of the cookie ministry;
- name of the organization that will receive the cookies;
- number of cookies they need to bake;
- request cookies be brought in non-returnable containers such as plastic food storage bags, empty bread bags, plastic margarine, or ice cream containers;
- day, date, and place to bring the cookies;
- your telephone number.

This information is also essential if you contact the people by telephone.

Help us bake cookies in the church kitchen.

Cookies are for _____

Please sign up for the month you will bake cookies. Four people are needed for each month.

Name _____
Phone _____
Month _____

For information call: _____
at _____

Please Bring Ingredients for the cookie pantry.

We are making chocolate chip cookies for
_____

Nursery (bed babies) . . . . Vanilla extract
Toddlers (ages 1-3) . . . . Salt
Preschool (ages 4-5) . . . . Soda
Children (grades 1-3) . . . . Brown sugar
Children (grades 4-5) . . . . Sugar
Youth . . . . Chocolate chips
Young Adults . . . . All purpose flour
Adult 1. . . . . Money for eggs & butter
Adult 11 . . . . Any ingredient
Adult 111. . . . . Any ingredient

Sunday School Teachers,
Please encourage your class members to bring their ingredients. You may want to mail reminders or call everyone to remind them to bring their ingredients.

We at _____ Church care about you. We hope you enjoy these cookies.

This is the day which the Lord hath made; we will rejoice and be glad in it (Psalm 118:24).

Cookies provided by
_____ Church

Someone at _____ church cares about you. Enjoy these cookies.

My Favorite Recipes from Hershey Foods
♥♥♥♥♥

Here are my favorite recipes that I use to bake cookies for the cookie ministry. I love to bake cookies, so I bake them every month. Sometimes I let my family have a few of these wonderful cookies, too. All of these recipes come directly from Hershey Foods Corporation, who has graciously permitted me to share my favorite cookie recipes with you in this book.

HERSHEY'S, REESE'S, SKOR, MINI CHIPS, and PERFECTLY CHOCOLATE are registered trademarks. Recipes courtesy of the Hershey Kitchens, and reprinted with permission of Hershey Foods Corporation.

©Hershey Foods Corporation

Oatmeal Brownie Drops
¾ cup sugar
½ cup (1 stick) butter or margarine, softened
2 eggs
1 teaspoon vanilla extract
1 cup all-purpose flour
½ cup HERSHEY'S cocoa
¼ teaspoon baking soda
1 cup quick-cooking rolled oats
1 cup HERSHEY'S MINI CHIPS Semi-Sweet Chocolate

Heat oven to 350°F. In large mixer bowl, beat together sugar and butter until well blended. Add eggs and vanilla; blend thoroughly. In small bowl, stir together flour, cocoa, and baking soda; add to butter mixture, blending thoroughly. Stir in oats and small chocolate chips. Drop by tablespoonfuls onto ungreased cookie sheet. Bake 7 to 8 minutes or until cookie begins to set. Do not overbake. Remove from cookie sheet to wire rack; cool completely. About 3½ dozen cookies.

Chocolate Oatmeal Cookies
1 cup (2 sticks) butter or margarine, softened
1½ cups granulated sugar
1 cup packed light brown sugar
2 eggs
2 teaspoons vanilla extract
1½ cups all-purpose flour
½ cup HERSHEY'S Cocoa or HERSHEY'S Premium European Style Cocoa
1 teaspoon baking soda
½ teaspoon salt
3 cups quick-cooking or regular rolled oats
½ cup chopped nuts

Heat oven to 350°F. In large mixer bowl, beat butter, granulated sugar, and brown sugar until light and fluffy; blend in eggs and vanilla. Stir together flour, cocoa, baking soda, and salt; gradually add to butter mixture, mixing well. Stir in oats and nuts. (Batter will be stiff.) Drop by rounded tablespoonfuls onto ungreased cookie sheet. Bake 11 to 12 minutes or until set; cookies will be slightly moist in center. DO NOT OVERBAKE. Cool 1 minute; remove from cookie sheet to wire rack. Cool completely. About 4 dozen cookies.

Cocoa Oatmeal Treats
These easy, no-bake candy-cookies have been a favorite for generations.

2 cups sugar
½ cup (1 stick) butter or margarine
½ cup milk
⅓ cup HERSHEY'S Cocoa
⅓ cup REESE'S Creamy or Crunchy Peanut Butter
2½ cups quick-cooking rolled oats
½ cup chopped unsalted peanuts
2 teaspoons vanilla extract

In medium saucepan, combine sugar, butter, milk and cocoa. Cook over medium heat, stirring constantly, until mixture comes to rolling boil; boil and stir 1 minute. Remove from heat. Add oats, peanut butter, peanuts and vanilla; stir to mix well. Quickly drop mixture by heaping teaspoons onto wax paper or foil. Cool completely. Store in cool, dry place. About 4 dozen treats.

Reese's Chewy Chocolate Cookies

2 cups all-purpose flour
¾ cup HERSHEY'S Cocoa
1 teaspoon baking soda
½ teaspoon salt
1¼ cups (2½ sticks) butter or margarine, softened

2 cups sugar
2 eggs
2 teaspoons vanilla extract
1⅔ cups (10-ounce package) REESE'S Peanut Butter Chips

Heat oven to 350°F. In bowl, stir together flour, cocoa, baking soda, and salt. In large mixer bowl, beat butter and sugar until light and fluffy. Add eggs and vanilla; beat well. Gradually add flour mixture, beating well. Stir in chips. Drop by rounded teaspoonfuls onto ungreased cookie sheet. Bake 8 to 9 minutes. (Do not overbake; cookies will be soft. They will puff while baking and flatten while cooling.) Cool slightly; remove from cookie sheet to wire rack. Cool completely. About 4½ dozen cookies.

PAN RECIPE: Spread batter in greased 15½-by-10½-by-1-inch jelly-roll pan. Bake at 350°F, 20 minutes or until set. Cool completely in pan on wire rack; cut into bars. About 4 dozen bars.

ICE CREAM SANDWICHES: Prepare CHEWY CHOCOLATE COOKIES as directed; cool. Press small scoop of vanilla ice cream between flat sides of cookie. Wrap and freeze.

HIGH ALTITUDE DIRECTIONS
Increase flour to 2 cups plus 2 tablespoons
Decrease baking soda to ¾ teaspoon
Decrease sugar to 1⅔ cups
Add 2 teaspoons water with flour mixture
Bake at 350°F, 7 to 8 minutes
Yield increases to about 6 dozen.

HERSHEY'S Classic Chocolate Chip Cookies

This is HERSHEY'S famous recipe for traditional chocolate chip cookies.

2¼ cups all-purpose flour
1 teaspoon baking soda
½ teaspoon salt
1 cup (2 sticks) butter, softened
¾ cup granulated sugar
¾ cup packed light brown sugar
1 teaspoon vanilla extract
2 eggs
2 cups (12-oz. pkg.) HERSHEY'S Semi-Sweet Chocolate Chips
1 cup chopped nuts (optional)

Heat oven to 375°F. Stir together flour, baking soda and salt. In large bowl, beat butter, granulated sugar, brown sugar and vanilla with electric mixer until creamy. Add eggs; beat well. Gradually add flour mixture, beating well. Stir in chocolate chips and nuts, if desired. Drop by rounded teaspoons onto ungreased cookie sheet. Bake 8 to 10 minutes or until lightly browned. Cool slightly; remove from cookie sheet to wire rack. Cool completely. About 5 dozen cookies.

PAN RECIPE: Spread batter in greased 15½ x10½ x1-inch jelly-roll pan. Bake at 375°F. 20 minutes or until lightly browned. Cool completely; cut into bars. About 4 dozen bars.

HERSHEY'S "PERFECTLY CHOCOLATE" CHOCOLATE CHIP COOKIES: Simply add 1/3 cup HERSHEY'S Cocoa to your favorite chocolate chip cookie recipe.

SKOR & CHOCOLATE CHIP COOKIES: Use 1 cup finely chopped SKOR bars and 1 cup HERSHEY'S Semi-Sweet Chocolate Chips in place of 2 cups chocolate chips; omit nuts. Drop and bake as directed.

ICE CREAM SANDWICH: Press one small scoop vanilla ice cream between two cookies.

HIGH ALTITUDE DIRECTIONS (classic cookies):
Increase flour to 2⅔ cups.
Decrease baking soda to ¾ teaspoon.
Decrease granulated sugar to ⅔ cup.
Decrease packed light brown sugar to ⅔ cup.
Add ½ teaspoon water with flour.
Bake at 375°F, 5 to 7 minutes or until top is light golden with golden brown edges.

Cookie Carriers

You can deliver cookies in any kind of containers; however, they will be more impressive when delivered in a decorative bag, box, container, or basket. People who receive the cookies will see that you took an extra step to brighten their day. The handmade carriers shown here require a minimum of expense and time. Look around your kitchen for boxes, baskets, bags, cardboard and plastic containers, large glass jars, and cookie tins. The cookie carriers that I make can be reused, bringing a smile even after all the cookies are gone. As your ministry grows and you gain experience, you will think of many fun and decorative ways to deliver your cookies.

A group of women in my church always volunteer to make cookie carriers for the cookie ministry. They get together as a group and have a great time working on their crafts together. I always use recycled household items to make the carriers. The women in the group collect the items and save them for making cookie carriers.

Show these ideas and directions to your Sunday School teachers, children's department directors, and others who like to do simple crafts. Let volunteers choose the cookie carriers that they want make. Just let them know how many carriers you need and when you need them. Some women's groups, youth groups, or children's groups may want to take this on as a monthly project. This project could begin a new ministry group in your church. Crafts are a popular topic among some women. Those who enjoy making things with their hands may decide to branch out and establish a community ministry of their own.

Choose someone from your group who will be in charge of getting cookie carriers made. She will be able to answer the crafters' questions and assist them with obtaining necessary supplies. In some cases, this person will be the one to gather the crafters together to work on crafts. In situations where crafters prefer to make their cookie carriers at home, she will simply need to collect the completed carriers and deliver them to the cookie ministry at the appropriate time.

Most of the cookie carriers shown here can be completed in an hour. You may need to enlist only three or four people to make carriers each month. Or, you may prefer to have a group activity with a whole Sunday School department making dozens of containers at one time. Try to plan and coordinate your projects. If you enlist only three people, and you need 50 carriers, it may take several days before you have enough. Always plan so that the crafters will have plenty of time to complete their carriers.

Anyone in the church can make cookie carries. Consider getting the men in on these projects, and enlist children and teenagers whenever possible. This may become such a popular project that the group chooses a catchy name for itself such as Cookies and Carriers, or Bags, Boxes, and Baskets. You can have a successful cookie ministry without making cookie carriers, but everyone; church members and cookie recipients; like the additional, cheerful touch that decorative cookie carriers provide.

Volunteers who decide to make cookie carriers at church, will need a large room for work and fellowship. If possible, find a room that has a sink in it. They will need one or two long tables (more if there is a large group of crafters) set up near an electrical outlet, in case you use glue guns for your projects. Have several extension cords available, also.

When the volunteer crafters have agreed upon a time, add it to the church calendar. If appropriate, arrange for the room to be set up the day before the crafters get together. Crafters may want to make this a regular weekly or monthly meeting. Consider the first Monday or second Tuesday of each month.

Allow the crafters to choose the time of their meeting, but try to make it consistent if you choose monthly craft times. If most of the crafters do not work outside the home, weekday mornings may be best for this kind of project. Older men and women who do not drive at night might prefer to meet during the morning. Mothers with children in school might find this a good time, also. If most of your crafters work outside the home or are teenagers and children who attend school, consider having a regular craft time one Saturday each month.

A nursery is essential for crafters who must bring their small children with them. The children will be safe and happy while their parents focus their attention on making cookie carriers. Talk with the nursery director about providing a nursery during the craft time. If your church does not have a nursery staff, ask the crafters if they can each pay a small fee for someone to keep the nursery. Another alternative is for the crafters to take turns keeping the nursery. If your crafters agree on a meeting time at night, try to schedule the time so that children have other activities such as children's choir.

Allow the crafters to be responsible for obtaining the necessary supplies to make the cookie carriers. They may want to ask Sunday School departments to help out with the cost of glue, stickers, ribbon, and plastic bags. The basic items such as oatmeal boxes and plastic fruit baskets can be collected from their homes, or they may ask others in the church to help them collect such items. As the cookie ministry grows, you may ask that money be designated in the church budget for these kinds of items.

If you need church members to help collect items, make posters advertising the items needed and how they will be used. Include on this poster when and where to bring the items, and a name and telephone number of a contact person for information about the cookie ministry. Make a sample cookie carrier and put it near the poster.

Ask people who sew and do other kinds of craft projects to clean out their supply closets. You can use leftover ribbon, yarn, and so forth, for many of the cookie carriers shown here. See if you can find a wallpaper store that is giving away old wallpaper books. Ask church members to recycle their old Christmas and greeting cards for this project. Look around you. There are many place to find inexpensive craft items to make decorative cookie carriers.

Most of these cookie carriers can be reused after the cookies are gone. The people who receive your gifts will have a lasting reminder of the cookies and love that you and your church gave to them.

✂ Paper Twist Basket
Materials needed:
- oatmeal box (42-ounce)
- tape measure or ruler
- Utility knife
- scissors
- clothespins
- craft glue or glue gun and glue sticks
- 3 yards paper twist (1½ yards each of 2 alternating colors)
- poster board (any color, new or used)

Use a tape measure or ruler to measure the height of the box. Start from the bottom and measure up to find the center of the box. Mark a small dot, so you will know where to cut the box. Cut the box in half with a utility knife or other sharp knife. Spread out one strip of colored paper twist. This will make the vertical design. Fold the paper width in half and cut down the center. Now the paper twist will be 2 inches wide. Measure the paper twist and cut 6 strips, 18-inches long. Turn the box upside down and lay two strips on the bottom in a crisscross (X) shape. Then, bring each strip to the top edge of the box. Turn about one inch of paper twist to the inside of the box. Use clothespins to secure the paper twist onto top rim of box. Now place remaining strips across the bottom of box in a crisscross fashion to fill in gaps. Secure top edges with clothespins as done previously. Make sure all inside edges are the same length. When all vertical strips are in place, they will completely cover the sides of the box, with no gap between each strip.

Measure and cut one yard of the second color of paper twist. Fold paper width in half and cut on the fold. Now you will have two pieces that are 1 yard (36-inches) long and 2-inches wide. Cut each of these pieces in half and you will have 4 pieces of paper twist that are 18-inches long. Take clothespin off one piece of paper twist at the rim of the box. Pull paper twist down to bottom of the box. Take the second color of paper twist and place it horizontally behind the vertical strip you just pulled away from the box. Start at the bottom of the box. Secure one end of the horizontal paper twist with glue to the box in such a way that the raw edge is behind the vertical strip. Then, weave this piece over and under the remaining vertical paper twist strips. Complete the circle back to where you begin weaving, then glue paper twist ends together to the box. Make sure this glue point is behind the vertical strip. Remove clothespins each time as needed. Stretch vertical paper twist piece back to the rim of the box and replace clothespins after each step of paper weaving. Remove clothespin from adjoining vertical strip of paper twist, pull it away from the box and weave another horizontal strip of paper twist. Replace the vertical strip of paper twist to the rim of the box with clothespin. Repeat around the box until pattern is complete. When the entire box is covered it will look like a colorful woven basket.

Cut a 12-inch piece of paper twist, and spread it out. (Do not cut down center.) The paper twist will be 4-inches wide and 12-inches long. Measure a piece of poster board and cut a piece 12-inches long and 1fi-inches wide. Lay paper twist flat on table and lay poster board in center of paper twist. Fold each side of paper twist to the center of the poster board and glue paper twist to poster board. The covered poster board will be the handle. Place each end of the handle about one inch down on the inside rim. Glue handle in place. Now cut a piece of paper twist the size of the inside perimeter of the box. This will be the remaining strip of the horizontal color. Glue this to the inside of box to cover the cut off edges of paper twist and make the inside neat and attractive.

Fill small plastic bags with cookies and put in the basket. Women or teenage girls would appreciate this basket filled with cookies and love. The basket can be used later for holding cotton balls in bathroom, bedroom, or baby's room. Red and green are festive for Christmas baskets, however, paper twist comes in a variety of colors. Try pastel colors for spring baskets.

✂ Christmas Card Basket

Materials needed:
- scissors
- ruler
- glue or spray adhesive
- stapler
- 4 Christmas cards (cards should fit the size of box)
- 1 square or rectangular box (size of cards)
- poster board (Christmas color)

Measure box to find the center of the front and back. Cut 2 strips of poster board 1½-by-12-inches for the handle. Glue the 2 strips together and trim edges neatly. When completely dry, staple or glue the ends of the handle to center front and back of box. Cut Christmas cards apart. Use only the front picture part of each card. If necessary, cut each card to fit the box. Glue a card to each side of the box.

Wrap cookies in plastic wrap. Gather wrap in center and tie with yarn, ribbon, or paper twist. You may choose to package cookies in plastic bag. Baskets can be used to hold Christmas cards after the cookies are eaten. A person who is homebound or lives alone will appreciate a Christmas basket of cookies.

Consider using other kinds of greeting cards to make baskets for other occasions. Birthday cards would be appropriate for some cookie ministry projects.

✂ Christmas Cookie Canister

Materials needed:
oatmeal box (42-ounce)
2 plastic lids (to fit the oatmeal box)
scissors
iron
tape measure
spray adhesive
small Christmas flower pick, decoration, or stick on bow
¼ yard Christmas fabric or any small print fabric
paper-backed fusible web (10-by-18-inches)

Use tape measure to measure the height and circumference of oatmeal box. Cut fabric and webbing material the size (height and circumference) of box plus 1 inch. Iron webbing onto fabric following manufacturer's directions. Spray adhesive on box and quickly cover box with fabric, overlapping ends in back. Smooth out any wrinkles with hands. Put one plastic lid on the bottom of the box and the other on the top. Glue a decoration or bow on the top of the box. Tape a cookie calling card to the inside top of the box. (A sample of this card is in the chapter titled Samples and Announcements.)

Fill the canister with cookies. This canister is appropriate for someone who has a family member in the hospital during the Christmas season. The person can reuse the canister year after year and be reminded of the gift of cookies and love that your church provided.

Consider using smaller boxes with different fabric patterns and decorations for giving at other times of the year.

✂ Wrapping Paper Basket

Materials needed:
- English muffin container
- utility knife
- scissors
- pencil
- gift-wrapping paper
- tape measure
- spray adhesive
- hot glue gun and glue sticks
- poster board or any kind of cardboard for handle

One container will make two baskets. Measure the height of the container and mark the center with a pencil. Use this mark as your cutting guide. Half of the container will have a bottom. Glue the plastic top to the other half to make a bottom.

Lay one half aside. Measure the height and circumference of the first container with a tape measure. Add 1 inch to height (for turning paper under at top and bottom) and ½ inch to the circumference (for overlapping in the back). Cut paper according to your measurements. Spray container with spray adhesive. Allow ½ inch at top and bottom for turning the paper under at each end. Quickly place wrapping paper on sprayed container. Carefully press paper with your hands to prevent wrinkles.

Cut 2 pieces 1-by-12-inches to make the handle. Glue these pieces together. Measure paper and cut a piece large enough to cover both sides of the handle. Spray adhesive on poster board and quickly cover both sides of poster board with paper. Put glue on outside edges of handle. Glue handle to the inside of the box. Make sure the edges of the handle touch the bottom of the box.

Fill small plastic bags with cookies. This is an appropriate container for women or teenage girls. Basket can be reused to hold small soaps or an arrangement of flowers.

✂ Shoe Box Basket

Materials needed:
- 1 shoe box
- tape measure
- yardstick
- scissors
- spray adhesive or craft glue
- hot glue gun and glue sticks
- poster board (3-inches-by-22-inches)
- 1 sheet of gift-wrapping paper (20-inches-by-2½-feet)

Measure the height of the shoe box with the tape measure; add 1½ inches. This is the width needed for the wrapping-paper strip. Measure the distance around the shoe box. This is the length needed for the wrapping-paper strip.

Lay wrapping paper upside down on a table and measure and mark the size of the strip. Use the yardstick as a straight edge to mark a straight line where to cut out your strip of wrapping paper. If your paper is not long enough, cut and glue an extra piece of paper to the side of the box. (Use the corners as your splice point.)

Use spray adhesive or craft glue to attach the paper to the box. Align the paper with the bottom edge of the box and the extra 1½ inch will stick up past the top of the box. Wrap paper around box and make neat sharp corners as you turn the paper around each corner. After all sides are glued, clip each of the four top corners at the corner fold. Then, turn each top strip down toward the inside of the box and glue securely.

Now make the handle from poster board. Measure and cut two 1½-by-22 strips.

Glue the two strips together for strength. Put glue on the handle and cover with wrapping paper. Measure the box to find the center of the side you want to place the handle. Place end of handle all the way down to the bottom of the box. Use a hot glue gun to glue handle inside of box.

Fill a large plastic bag full of cookies and put them in your basket. The families at a Ronald McDonald House or in a church's transitional house will appreciate the basket full of cookies. The basket can be reused for holding stationery, notepads, envelopes, all occasion cards, pencils, and books of stamps. Providing these supplies can be an additional ministry of a church.

✂ Strawberry Baskets

Materials needed:
- 1 clean plastic strawberry basket
- 1 chenille stem (any color)
- craft glue or hot glue gun and glue sticks
- scissors
- tape measure
- 1 or 2 yards of ribbon (⅜-inch or ⅞-inch widths) may use scraps of different colors

Cut strips of ribbon about ½-inch longer than the perimeter of the basket. The width and number of strips will vary according to the size of your baskets. Some have three rows, where others may have only two rows. Weave ribbon in and out of the holes around the basket. Overlap ribbon and put a dab of glue between ribbon edges. Press ribbon with fingers and hold firmly for a few seconds. Place one end of chenille stem at the center front of the basket; bend and twist into a loop. Do the same with the other end of the chenille stem at the center back of the basket, forming a handle. Make sure the loops are twisted securely so the handle will support the weight of the basket. Cut a 14-inch piece of ribbon. Put a dab of glue at one end and wrap around the chenille stem. Be sure to cover twisted area well. Cut two pieces of ribbon about 10-inches long to make small bows. Place bows on each side at the edge of the handle.

Fill small plastic bags with cookies. This makes an ideal Easter basket for children in a children's home or homeless shelter. You can put Easter grass in the basket before adding the cookies. The basket can be reused for hair bows, ribbons, or barrettes.

✂ Paper Bag Baskets
Materials needed:
- brown lunch bag
- stapler and staples
- scissors
- ruler or tape measure
- glue
- pictures of cookies (cut from magazines)

Measure about 1½ inch from top of bag. Cut off this strip to make the handle for your bag. Fold bag in half to the inside until the top touches the bottom of bag. Now your bag will have a double thickness for additional support.

Measure center of front and back of bag. Fold handle in half vertically for double thickness. Staple ends of handle to center front and back of bag. Make a fringe around top of bag by cutting slits about 1-inch down and ¼-inch apart around bag. Cut pictures of cookies from magazines and glue to front of bag.

Fill a small plastic bag with cookies and place in the paper bag basket. These baskets are good gifts for disabled people. The baskets can be reused to hold crayons, pencils, note paper, scissors, and other school supplies.

✂ Brown Paper Bags
Materials needed:
- brown paper lunch bags
- bright colored markers
- scissors
- glue
- cookie cutters
- hole punch
- 18 inches of yarn or ribbon
- construction paper or poster board
- used greeting cards (Christmas or any occasion)
- used gift-wrapping paper (new or used)

Bag 1. Cut pictures from greeting cards or gift-wrapping paper and glue to paper bag. These pictures can be seasonal or for any occasion.

Bag 2. Cut out Bible verses or inspirational poems and glue to paper bags. Save your old Sunday School books so you can cut out the Bible verses. Inspirational messages and Bible verses are also found in greeting cards.

Bag 3. Cut out objects from bright, colorful construction paper or poster board and glue them to paper bags. Cookie cutters are great to use in tracing your patterns. You may choose to use holiday patterns as hearts for Valentine's Day or a Christmas tree for Christmas. You can write Bible verses on the objects. Be sure writing is neat and legible.

BAG 4. Sponge paint bags with various shapes of sponges and colors of paint.

BAG 5. Use markers to draw the face of the animal on the bag. Cut ears of appropriate animal from construction paper or poster board and attach to the bag.

Fill bags with cookies to share the love of your church with others. This is a good gift for the men and women at homeless shelters. Children at the shelter will love animal bags.

Consider decorating large grocery bags to make carriers for your smaller bags.

✂ Plastic Bags

Materials needed:
- stickers
- index cards
- markers
- plastic bags
- scraps of bright ribbon, yarn, or paper twist

Use bags with twist-ties or the self-sealing bags. Gallon-, quart-, pint-, or sandwich-sized bags are ideal for cookies. Glue stickers to the bags. Religious stickers are a silent witness to the person receiving the cookies. Use bright bows, ribbons, yarns, or paper twist where appropriate. Use colorful markers to write Bible verses or inspirational messages on index cards, and staple these to the bags.

These make good gifts for college students. The sandwich-sized or pint-sized bags can be used for individual bags of cookies. Gallon-sized bags hold enough cookies for a large group.

✂ Heart-shaped Baskets

Materials needed:
- pencil
- scissors
- glue
- hole punch
- 1 page of wallpaper from a wallpaper book (small print patterns)
- 12-inch ribbon (¼- or ½-inch width)

Trace pattern on wallpaper and cut out two heart shapes. Measure about 2 inches from top of hearts and mark a dot with a pencil. On one heart put glue around sides and bottom of heart, from dot to dot. Place the other heart on top, and press the two hearts together. Let glue dry. Punch a hole in the top center of the hearts. Pull ribbon through the holes and tie a knot in each end on the inside of the heart, making a handle.

A heart-shaped basket filled with cookies will be a special treat for girls who live in shelters or temporary homes with their mothers.

✂ Christmas Card Stocking
Materials needed:
- 1 large Christmas card or red poster board
- 1 piece of red or green poster board (size of card) for back of stocking
- hole punch
- 1 yard yarn
- scissors
- white, unlined paper for tracing
- pencil

Trace stocking with pencil onto white paper. Cut out stocking pattern. Use pattern to cut one stocking from card and one stocking from poster board. Put stocking together, be sure picture is on front. Hold stocking together and punch holes about one inch apart around stocking.

Sew stocking with yarn. Put yarn in the first hole at the top of stocking. Tie a knot on the back of stocking. Sew yarn over and under remaining holes around stocking. Tie remaining yarn to beginning hole of stocking, making a handle. Put four to six cookies in a small plastic bag and put the bag in the stocking.

You can also use poster board in Christmas colors to make your stocking. Decorate the stocking with Christmas stickers or pictures cut from Christmas cards or Christmas wrapping paper.

✂ Cookie Cans
Materials needed:
- shortening or coffee cans
- self-adhesive plastic or wallpaper
- glue as necessary
- ruler
- scissors

Wash cans in hot, soapy water to remove all grease or coffee. Let can dry thoroughly. Measure length and width of the can. Add ½ inch to the width and 1 inch to the length. Cut self-adhesive plastic or wallpaper to match the measurements you have calculated. Cover the cans with the paper, using the self-adhesive plastic or glue. Fold over about ½-inch at top of can and turn under about ½-inch at the bottom of the can. Add a colorful kitchen pattern to make a special cookie container.

A can of cookies will be a warm welcome to a new church family. Greet your new neighbors with a can of cookies and invite them to church.

Baskets
Baskets are a good way to deliver your cookies. These baskets can be new or used, if in good condition. Sometimes you can find good baskets at garage sales or thrift stores. Place a paper or cloth napkin in the basket and fill it with cookies. You may also put cookies in a plastic bag or plastic wrap, and then put them in the basket. Make a ribbon, lace, or paper twist bow and attach to the basket.

Large 32-ounce Plastic Cups
Save your cups from fast-food restaurants for another type of cookie carrier. Fill the cup with cookies, and cover the top of the cup with a small piece of plastic wrap. Stretch a rubber band around the top of the cup to hold the plastic wrap in place.

Cookie Tins
These tins often have bright, cheerful pictures on top. They keep cookies fresh, and can be reused in many ways. Look for inexpensive tins at garage sales and dollar stores.

Throw-away Pie Plates
Save your foil pie plates after you eat the pie. Arrange the cookies on the pie plate and cover with plastic wrap. Colored plastic wraps make a pretty plate. Try using a large piece of plastic wrap and gathering it at the top. Then, use ribbon or yarn to wrap to make a pretty bow.

Thanks

♥♥♥♥♥

I want to thank God for opening the many doors of opportunities for me to serve Him in my cookie ministries. I want to say a special thanks to everyone who had a part in helping to make these ministries possible. Without their support my ministries and book would not be possible.

Thanks to my pastors and the church staffs for their support and allowing me to lead a cookie ministry. Thanks to Margaret Owens, our education secretary, who faithfully sends out cookie letters each month to the women who volunteered to bake cookies.

Thanks to the directors of the various organizations for allowing our church to give cookies to the many people who are a part of their groups.

Thanks to each person who bakes cookies. Without your willingness to help these ministries would not be possible.

Thanks to each person who helped deliver the cookies to the various groups of people. This is a very special part of the ministry.

Thanks to my WMU Mission Action group for making individual bags of cookies for the men at the homeless shelter.

A special thanks to my husband, Ray Campbell, who supports me in all my missions endeavors. Without his computer help, support, and encouragement, *Giving Cookies and Love* would not be possible.

I also wish to thank the Hershey Foods Corporation for graciously granting their permission to publish recipes.

About the Author
♥♥♥♥♥

Grace Earline Campbell is Woman's Missioanry Union director and leader of a cookie ministry at East Brent Baptist Church, Pensacola, Florida. She has led mission action conferences for the Pensacola Bay Baptist Association and Women on Mission organizations.

She served 15 years as a leader in the Choctaw Baptist Association in Fort Walton Beach, Florida. Her areas of service included Girls in Action director, Acteens director, associational Acteens director, Baptist Women president, and WMU director. She is a former assignment writer for *Accent* magazine, a monthly publication of Woman's Missionary Union, and has led conferences for Acteens.

Missions involvement is important to her family. Her husband, Ray, is supportive in all her missions endeavors. Although his name is not on every page, he is the co-author. This book is the result of a husband and wife working together as a team. They have two daughters, Sharon Wilharm and Connie Mashburn, and three grandchildren, Jonathan and Hannah Mashburn and Brittany Wilharm. Sharon is Acteens director for her church and Pensacola Bay Baptist association. She is also a writer for *Accent* magazine. Connie and her husband are field assistance missionaries in Indiana.